# Concertante in G Major

## In Three Movements for Solo Piano with Piano Accompaniment

## Dennis Alexander

## Contents

*Music Teachers National Association*
*and*
*Montana State Music Teachers Association*
*1996 Commissioned Work*

# Concertante in G Major

## I.

Dennis Alexander

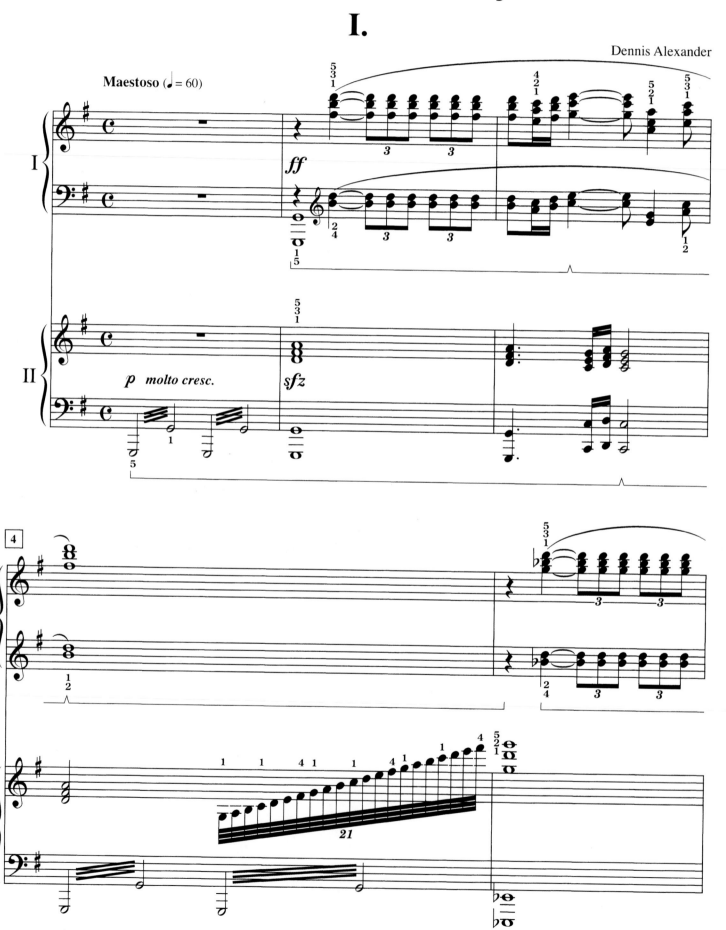

poco a poco accelerando

poco a poco accelerando

**Allegro gioioso\*** ( ♩ = 120–126)

*Gioioso* means "joyous" or "cheerful."

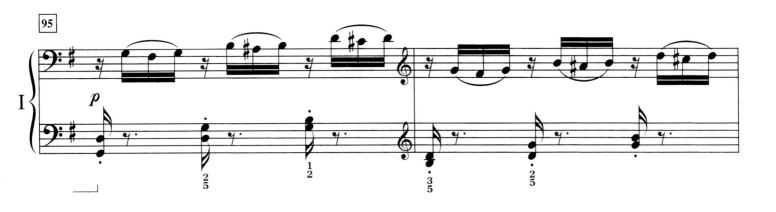

**Tempo I** ( ♩ = 120–126)

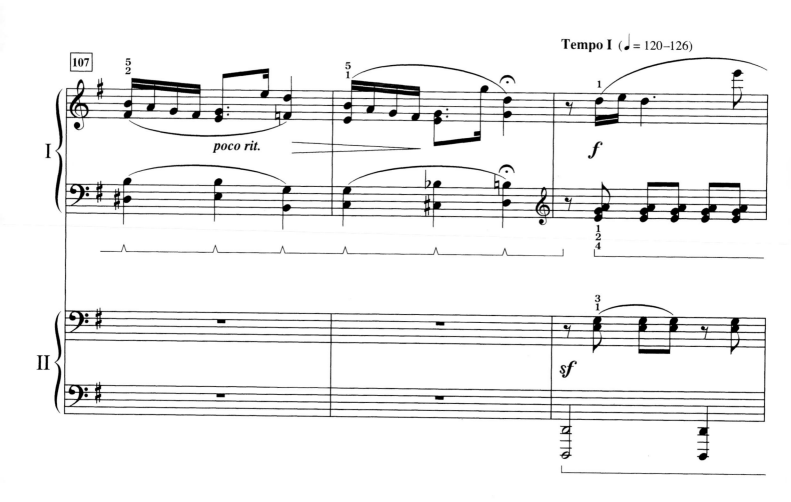

# II.

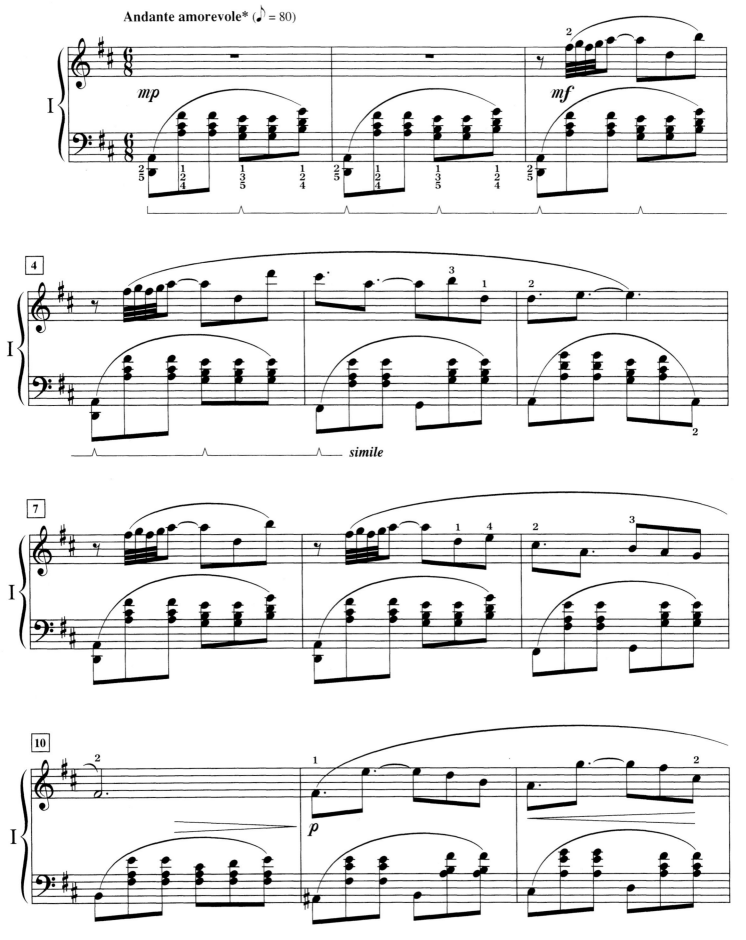

*Amorevole* means "amiable."

# III.

RONDO

**Allegro giocoso** (♩ = 138)